Praise for 40 L__.

Why waste your time worrying for a loved one, when you could spend that same time praying powerful prayers of salvation, breakthrough, and blessings instead? Join Eric Sprinkle and Laura Shaffer as they give you the blueprint for prayers that make a world of difference.

> Linda Evans Shepherd, bestselling author of *Praying God's Promises* and *Praying Through Every Emotion*.

I've been doing the *40 Day Prayer Guides — Praying for Someone's Salvation* for about 2 weeks now and it's such a huge blessing. The prayers are wonderful, and working through each day's prayers has definitely been a blessing to me each morning. I am actively seeking time with the person I am praying for as a result of praying for him and we have had a lot of fun... plus it has laid a groundwork of trust for God to work in through our conversations. In fact, my husband and I are praying through the book together, for the same person. I'll pray during my morning quiet time, then snap a photo of the prayer and send it to my husband at work where he'll pray for it. I can't believe how close it's making us feel doing this 40 day journey together! I was telling my best friend about the change that's taking place in my heart, anticipating the change the Lord is bringing to my prayer subject's heart, and she shared how she needs something like this for one of her loved ones. Now she has the book and is praying. God is at work!

> Robin Shear, professional Joy Coach, author of the JOY BITES blog & an upcoming book about finding joy despite difficult circumstances. (www.joytotheworldcoaching.com)

Thoroughly comprehensive, practical, clear, inspiring and helpful. HIGHLY recommend.

There was so little information I could find about this book, that I finally ordered it hardly knowing what to expect or anything much about the author(s). However, within moments of receipt I had real heart assurance that this was written by real Jesus disciples and going to be an invaluable aid to praying for loved ones.

Laura Shaffer along with Eric Sprinkle, has used her gentle, comprehensive and long-ranging experience of intercessory prayer to compose a guiding book which is user-friendly, encouraging and hope-inspiring. Hang on in there. Keep praying, keep trusting and watch for answers to prayer 'better than you could ask or even think'. (Ephesians 3:20)

> Early Amazon Reviewer

40 DAY PRAYER GUIDES

Praying a Blessing for Someone

Powerful day-by-day prayers inviting God to Bless their life.

Eric Sprinkle and Laura Shaffer

Adventure Experience Press
"Fanning the flame within"

Praying a Blessing for Someone: Powerful day-by-day prayers inviting God to Bless their life.

Copyright ⓐ 2021 Eric Sprinkle and Laura Shaffer

All photos by Eric Sprinkle
Cover and interior design by Robin Black

ISBN: 978-1-7322694-3-9

Published by Adventure Experience Press in partnership with the fine folks at EA Books Books Publishing, a division of Living Parables of Central Florida, Inc. a 501c3

AdventureExperience.net
EABooksPublishing.com

DEDICATION

Laura—To my three sons, Scott, Ian and Collin who are three of God's most amazing blessings in my life and who have taught me the blessing, the value and the necessity of prayer.

Eric—To Ting Sun, friend, foodie and fellow adventurer. You are missed for sure and the ripple effect of the blessing you were continues to impact all our lives. I miss our talks and crazy adventures girl, but the final letter you wrote me from your hospital bed is a blessing I'll never forget.

ACKNOWLEDGEMENTS

- To Robin Black, Rebecca Ford, and the team at EA Books that helped us create, format, and publish this book in record time.
- Hugs and high fives to Debbie "Queen of Resilience" Hardy for jumping in and making all our edits happen.
- Eric also thanks "Trail Runner Jenna," for jumping in on a totally impromptu photo shoot out in Utah one day. Hey look, two months later, you're an Adventure Cover Model now, girl!
- Thank you to Laura's friends Matt and Dawn and Lynn who had life-changing circumstances, which relocated them across the country and prompted me to pray 40 days for them. Many of their needs are reflected in this book. I miss you all.
- Thank you to Bette, a gifted teacher and literacy specialist who provided input and feedback on scriptures, prayer content, and readability.
- I owe a debt of gratitude to my amazing prayer partners over the years who have been a blessing in my life, teaching me how to pray by example through our Torah group, Moms in Prayer groups, Community groups, and Bible studies.
- Extra special thanks go to Cathy and Michelle—my 40 Day partners who prayed with me through the "40 Days—Blessing" prayers. Their encouragement and suggestions were invaluable.
- Lastly and always, to our Gracious Lord God, who not only hears our prayers, but also blesses us far beyond what we could ever dare to ask or even hope to imagine.

Soli Deo Gloria indeed.

Introduction to 40 Days

Let's face it, our gracious Lord God has a thing for 40 days. Forty days of rain to flood the earth, 40 days spent in the wilderness before Jesus started his ministry, 40 days before the clock ran down on Nineveh to return to Him. Over and over, we see 40 days as the time frame God uses for major changes in people and circumstances.

Now, if I asked you to think of one person in your life who you want to see blessed, who immediately comes to mind?

Could this be the time to pray for God to bless them in a way you maybe never have before? To start your own personal 40-day prayer journey?

God loves it when we talk to and share with Him through prayer. Share our thoughts, our fears, our celebrations, and concerns. The Bible tells us it's our prayers and petitions, with thanksgiving, that God uses to bring us peace (Phil 4:6-7). Jesus himself told the disciples that sometimes when casting out demons only prayer will do the trick (Mark 9:29).

Maybe it's just me, but I get the feeling that I've vastly underestimated just how powerful prayer can be—and maybe you've felt that way too?

So, let's change it up. Let's make beautiful, Bible-based, laser-focused prayers a part of our daily routine for the next 40 days. Prayers for just one person. And instead of trying to think of the words, we'll use some of the most wonderful, powerful, stirring prayers you've ever heard, from our new mutual friend, Laura.

Let's read her prayers and make them our own. Let's pray them silently or aloud, inserting the name of the person that kept coming to mind. Don't worry, that'll be almost automatic by the time you get to Day 4.

What if we add a second person to pray for? What if we invite someone else to pray with us too? What if we invite a group of friends to join us on this 40-day prayer journey? All lifting up the same person, plans and ideas to Him, asking together for the Almighty to change that person's life. To reveal Himself. To call them to Him. To bless them.

Our Heavenly Father loves hearing our requests to Him through prayer. He loves blessing us with gifts too, often far more than we could ever ask or imagine.

I wonder what He wants to do in the life of that someone you know.

I say we find out.

It's time to turn the page and begin a 40-day journey, focused on praying blessing on the person you've chosen, one that's most certainly going to impact them, and you as well.

Are you ready?

Let's do this.

Blessing

I believe everyone desires to be blessed. I truly do. But many people did not grow up receiving a blessing. Or never learned how to give a blessing to others. The overused "Bless you" when someone sneezes carries little meaning anymore.

In Old Testament times, before a Hebrew father died, he spoke blessings over his sons as a way of passing on the leadership and possessions of the family.

Culturally, practicing Jewish parents recite a blessing over their children every Shabbat (Sabbath) at Friday dinner.

Both of these have a prophetic piece to them, as well as words of favor resting on the receiver.

Even before that, God blessed His creation of man and woman. It was an empowerment for them to be all He created them to be; a release from any and all restrictions or limitations preventing them from reaching their potential to participate in their divine purpose.

In Hebrew, the verb form "to bless" means "to kneel," while the noun translated as "blessing" means "a gift or present." So the concept is to bring or receive a gift or present, something of value, while kneeling out of respect.

The one who receives a blessing is changed, energized, empowered and enabled by the gift or the words of blessing.

Lord God, would You bless each one of us right now? Bless every reader as they read or speak this prayer, with the full definition of the meaning of the Hebrew word for bless:

> Heavenly Father, infuse us, fill us, permeate us, saturate us with unlimited potential to achieve all You would invite us to do that will glorify You and bring honor to Your Name.
>
> Release us from any restriction or limitation, whether physical, mental, emotional, spiritual, psychological, social, financial or personal that would prevent us or hold us back from becoming all You created us to be.
>
> Empower, energize and enable us to reach the fullness of our divine purpose.
>
> We kneel before You in receiving this divine blessing. Amen

This expanded definition of the Hebrew verb bless comes from Bill Bullock, The Rabbi's Son. Find him on www.biblicallifestylecenter.org.[1]

---

1. Bullock, Bill. 2009. "Torah Naso: Numbers 6:24-27." Torah Study Written Archives. https://biblicallifestylecenter.org/uploads/bill/pdfs/Naso/5781/35Chamishi81.pdf

How to Use this 40-Day Prayer Guide

Prayer pages:

The guide will give you one area of Blessing to pray each day for 40 days.

You can simply pray the prayer as it is, with the name of your person _____ in the blanks, or you can let the Holy Spirit guide you and use your own words.

Or these prayers can be a springboard for your prayer time as the Holy Spirit brings more things to mind as you pray.

For instance, there may be times when a particular problem or situation in the life of the person you're praying for will take precedence over a pre-planned agenda of prayer.

And there may be times when the Holy Spirit leads you to a different topic for blessing. Go for it.

Being flexible and sensitive to the Holy Spirit is the most important thing. Simply being intentional and consistent in your prayer time will help you be sensitive to the Holy Spirit.

Reflection Pages:

Every seven days the Guide will give you opportunities to:
- Write down your thoughts as you go along.
- Evaluate your progress.
- Look for ways God may be answering your prayers and thank Him.
- See how He is speaking to you personally about your prayer life, or how God might be leading you in your life.

There are, of course, many things you can pray to bless your friend. This is not meant to list or speak to all of them.

It will, however, help you be more intentional and consistent in praying. And by spending time in prayer, you will be open to the Spirit's leading. Learning to listen to the Holy Spirit guide you is most important.

It is my desire to help you grow in your prayer life as you pray for others. And that those you pray for will benefit from the answers to your prayers.

And that you will be blessed as you *Lean in and Learn from the Lord* through prayer.

Before Beginning

Reflections page . . .

Are you willing to set aside a few minutes each day to pray aloud for someone to receive a blessing?

We hope to encourage you and accompany you on your 40-day journey with day-by-day prayers. We also understand that sometimes things get in the way that are unavoidable. If you have to miss a day, simply pick up where you left off. You don't want to miss out on a blessing.

It may help to find a specific place or regular time of day to be sure you are being intentional and consistent in your praying (like when you first get up, or while exercising, on your way to work or during a break from work, or in a room or seat in your home at a certain time, or at a natural break in your daily routine).

When praying for another person, also called interceding in prayer, or intercession, there is wisdom in preparing yourself as well. Two areas are important:

1 — **Confession and Repentance** — The Bible tells us in Psalm 66:18, "If I had cherished sin in my heart, the Lord would not have listened." So it is important to take time to ask God to search your heart and show you any sin you need to confess and repent of before you move into interceding for someone.

God has promised that "If we confess our sins, He is faithful and just and will forgive us our sins and purify us from all unrighteousness" (1 John 1:9).

2 — **Spiritual Armor for Battle** — Ephesians tells us to be "Strong in the Lord and in His mighty power. Put on the full armor of God." 6:10-11. So we need to do that - name and pray on each piece before we pray for others.

Pages 111-113 in the Appendix at the back of this book will walk you through these steps.

Prayer tips

Are all prayers equal? It seems that God has listed some guidelines for us in Scripture that can either compromise or boost the effectiveness of our prayers.

There are even things that can cause Him to choose to step back or even disregard our prayers for a time. Yikes! Others are just the opposite, creating a multiplying effect on our prayers.

Have a look through and make sure nothing listed is going to get in your way over the next 40 days.

Some Biblical Guidelines

"The prayer of a righteous person is powerful and effective" (James 5:16).

Be sure you're following God and steering away from anything unrighteous or purposefully against God's ways for living. Holding grudges, being angry, indulging in wrongful thoughts or actions can all take away from the effectiveness of your 40-day journey.

"The eyes of the Lord are on the righteous, and his ears are attentive to their cry" (Psalm 34:15).

Exactly the opposite, we can rest assured we have God's complete attention when pursuing right living in our actions and choices.

"Then Jesus told his disciples a parable to show them that they should always pray and not give up" (Luke 18:1).

No worries there, you're going to be praying for the next 40 days, so you've got this!

"When you ask you do not receive, because you ask with wrong motives, that you may spend what you get on your pleasures" (James 4:3).

Okay, so praying for your boss to be blessed just so you get a promotion is not allowed, agreed?

"But your iniquities have separated you from your God; your sins have hidden his face from you, so that he will not hear" (Isaiah 59:2).

Again, let's be careful we don't have sin in our hearts that will get in the way of what we're asking. If we want to see the stars, let's get away from light pollution. If we want to talk to God, let's clear out the background noise and use a strong signal with four bars.

"This is the confidence we have in approaching God: that if we ask anything according to his will, he hears us" (1 John 5:14).

Let's all be sure we're asking for things in line with His will, His plans, His timing, and not our own. Trust that God is actively working to draw this person to Him, and bless them for His Glory, even if we're not seeing anything happening right away.

Additional ideas that can boost the impact of your praying

Pray these prayers out loud
Does it help God hear them better? No. Does it help you? You bet! Praying out loud helps you slow down and focus on the person and words you're praying - allowing time for the Holy Spirit to meet you in your prayer. And that can make a difference all on its own.

As the Holy Spirit brings additional things to mind when you're praying, pray those too
The Holy Spirit knows best what this person needs and what will bless them.

Pray the daily prayer multiple times a day
When you eat? Morning and evening? Or maybe whenever you start your car? When you think of the person you're praying for?

Pray for more than 1 person
What happens if you say two people's names for each prayer?

Pray this 40-Day journey with a friend,
Both of you, lifting up the same person in prayer. Or each of you praying for your own someone but checking in with each other on your journeys.

Consider fasting at some point during the journey
Giving up TV, social media, or even certain foods for a week during your journey will only serve to sharpen your spiritual focus!

Don't miss the Appendix Resources

Check out our Appendix at the back of this book for valuable resources you might need during your 40-day Journey. Whether that's how to specifically "armor up," explaining words like "repent," or how to hear God, we've got you covered.

Table of Contents

My Commitment

1 Timothy 2:1: *I urge, then, first of all, that petitions, prayers, intercession and thanksgiving be made for all people.*

In the Power of the Name of the Lord Jesus Christ, I am offering these prayers. Heavenly Father, I am trusting You to act and effect Your will during these next 40 days of prayer for _____. Draw them into a closer relationship with You by pouring out a blessing on them.

Father, I cannot even imagine all the forces that are currently influencing _____'s life. I know that the devil and the world and even our own flesh are at war with You and with all that is holy. Those forces seek to keep people away from You and from seeing the truth of Your work and blessing in their lives. Please be at work in _____'s life in ways that overcome any evil forces at work there.

Especially during these 40 days of prayer, be _____'s strength and spread Your protection over their body, mind and spirit. Watch over their physical health so no accident or illness sidelines them. Meet their emotional needs where relationships have been broken by betrayal, unmet expectations or dishonesty. Let them see truth and heal any spiritual wounds where they have been believing lies. Thank You for being at work in all these areas.

As for me, I will put on Your spiritual armor every day for these 40 days. (Ephesians 6:10-17) I will intercede for _____, asking that You bless them. And will "contend with those who contend with them and fight against those who fight against them" giving them victory over the enemies of their soul (Psalm 35:1).

Father, please help me in my commitment to pray daily. I give this 40-day journey to You. Lead me and teach me as I intercede for _____. I humbly ask for Your will to be done in and through _____'s life. Open up the storehouse of blessing, and let Your love and blessing pour over them to show them that You care, always. Amen

Recognition of Blessings from God

1 Corinthians 2:9: *However, as it is written: "What no eye has seen, what no ear has heard, and what no human mind has conceived"—the things God has prepared for those who love him—these are the things God has revealed to us by his Spirit.*

Heavenly Father, thank You in advance for every blessing and gift You pour out on _____.

It is my prayer that _____ would recognize and believe that all the blessings I am praying for in these 40 days come from You. Help them make the connection that it is Your favor that rests on them, not happenstance or fate, luck, or some other power in the universe.

When something good happens, it's such a human trait to think we ourselves made it happen. But when something bad happens, we try and find someone or something else to blame it on. Please let these blessings happen in a way, and impress it on _____, that they come straight from You: the Lover of their Soul, the Lifter of their head, the Creator of their very being.

Father, help me know if I should tell _____ that I am praying for You to bless their life during these 40 days or not. These blessings will demonstrate Your love for them in so many ways and meet many of their needs. But You know better than I whether they're in a place to hear that or not.

If I should not, then let these blessings add up on their own and point to You. Work in _____'s life in such a way they will see what is really happening.

If I should, show me the right time and the right circumstances to share with _____. Give me the right words to say, not trying to claim any credit for myself, but pointing to You in a way that honors You.

Let _____ Recognize whenever blessings come, that they come from You. Amen

Eternal Salvation or Spiritual Growth

If _____ is not a believer — Eternal Salvations

John 3:16: *For God so loved the world that he gave his one and only Son, that whoever believes in him shall not perish but have eternal life.*

Heavenly Father, would You be at work during these 40 days to soften _____'s heart and open their spiritual eyes and ears to the truth of who You are and Your amazing, unconditional, sacrificial love for them. Help them see how in that love, You sent Your Son, Jesus Christ as Messiah, to shed His blood and die on the cross as payment for their sin.

Show them that they are a sinner and need only accept that payment, believe that Jesus is Your Son who rose from the dead, and confess their desire to live a life pleasing to You.

Give _____ a hunger and thirst for spiritual truth. Lead them to the Bible and to someone who can help them understand it. Use the circumstances in their life, good or bad, to direct them to You. Reveal Yourself to _____ as Savior, Creator, and Lover of their soul in dreams, visions, or any other way You know will reach them.

Help me know if I should also get the *40-Day Prayer Guides: Praying for a Friend's Salvation* which is a more complete guide to pray for _____'s Salvation.

Let Salvation be a blessing from You, to _____. Amen

If _____ is a believer — Spiritual Growth

Colossians 2:7: *". . . rooted and built up in him, strengthened in the faith as you were taught."*

Heavenly Father, let these 40 days be a time of spiritual growth and awareness of who You are to _____ personally, and how You are involved with and at work in their life. Deepen Your relationship with _____ through prayer and give them a hunger and thirst to know Your Word better. Show them how to gain spiritual wisdom and understanding by seeking and hearing from You, and how to apply it to the circumstances and relationships in their life.

Help _____ find fellowship with other believers, discover the spiritual gifts You have given them, and find a place to use those gifts. Give them joy and boldness in their faith, and the opportunity and ability to share it with others.

When challenges and tests come, give _____ perseverance that will prove and purify their faith and help them become mature and complete, not lacking anything (James 1:4). Direct and encourage _____ as they seek Your wisdom and Your will for their life.

Let Spiritual Growth be a blessing from You, to _____. Amen

Peace

John 14:27: *Peace I leave with you; my peace I give you. I do not give to you as the world gives. Do not let your hearts be troubled and do not be afraid.*

Heavenly Father, give _____ Your peace right now in whatever circumstances they find themself. Thank You that You bring supernatural peace. It's not the peace the world gives, which depends on circumstances being favorable. But a peace amidst the storms of life even when things are not going well and we need help.

Calm whatever anxious thoughts _____ is having, and remind them they can bring anything to You - that no problem is too big or too small for You to handle. Let _____ cast any and every care they have on You. And let any worry trigger specific prayer to You for whatever they need and whatever You would show them.

Father, show _____ that You care for them, and that in Your great love You can offer them what no one else has to give. Give _____ peace in their tasks and decisions and a sense of peace in waiting when Your timetable is not what they expect or want. But also boldness to act when the time is right.

Calm _____ down and give them peace. Make the battles inside of them cease. Give them hope to carry on even when all the hope the world can give is gone. Thank You that You are the Prince of Peace.

Let Peace be a blessing from You, to _____ today. Amen

Identity

Psalm 139:14: *I praise you because I am fearfully and wonderfully made; your works are wonderful. I know that full well.*

Heavenly Father give _____ an awareness and an appreciation of the unique way You have created them. Thank You for giving _____ the positive traits that I see in them. Help _____ see themself through Your eyes, from Your perspective, and let that be the source of their sense of value and worth.

Help _____ understand the special personality, abilities, and experiences that have affected who they are today, and show them how those gifts will benefit them in the future. Teach _____ that their actions do not determine their identity, but that the identity You give them as a child of God determines their actions.

Do not allow _____ to define who they are or their worth by the world. Show _____ that they are more than the job they have or don't have, or the role they play in relationships. Jobs and relationships carry responsibilities and expectations. And too often our sense of worth suffers if we don't meet someone else's expected level of performance. But You, Father, love _____ regardless of what they do. You love _____ because of who they are.

Show _____ the great value You give them because they are Your child, Your creation, Your beloved son or daughter.

Scripture reveals:

    _____ *is chosen by You, holy and dearly loved,*

    _____ *is Your child,*

    _____ *is Your workmanship,*

    _____ *is fearfully and wonderfully made,*

    _____ *is the beloved who You rejoice over with singing!*

Let true Identity be a blessing from You to _____ today. Amen

Daily Bread

Matthew 6:11: *Give us today our daily bread.*

Heavenly Father, You have taught us to ask for our "daily bread" in The Lord's Prayer. I am asking for You to provide for _____'s daily bread: a supply of whatever they need, enough to meet the demands of their day.

If _____ has more than they need, they may think they are providing for themselves and don't need You. If they have too little, they can become angry, bitter and turn away from You; perhaps even turn down a dark path to get what they need.

Father, more than simply food, I am asking for You to grant _____ whatever is needed physically, emotionally and spiritually to get through each day these 40 days and beyond. Be there, close to them, providing everything the need of the moment calls for. It blows my mind that You, the Creator of the universe, are mindful of every need of every individual You have created every person on the entire planet! Those needs change every day, sometimes moment to moment. So I trust that You know exactly what they need and how to deliver it.

I trust You to see to _____'s practical, physical, professional, relational, mental, emotional, financial, and spiritual needs. _____ may not even realize what they are, but You do. And when You meet those needs, let them see You are the one graciously providing for and sustaining them.

I acknowledge that their very life is a gift from You, Father. Every breath they take, every beat of their heart is only by Your grace. I am so grateful for _____. And grateful to You for meeting their needs.

Let providing Daily Bread be a blessing from You, to _____ today. Amen

Good Health/Healing

Psalm 30:2: *LORD my God, I called to you for help, and you healed me.*

Heavenly Father, provide good health and healing to _____. Help their body work as it should, as You created it to work. If there's a physical illness or injury, be their Jehovah Rophe, their Healer. If an organ or body part has been damaged, bring healing to it. If they have been exposed to some disease, boost their immune system to fight it off.

If _____ is unaware of a sickness, weakness, or disease, bring it to their attention in the earliest stages and lead them to the right doctors, treatments, medications, or therapies that will work in concert with Your healing power. Do not let _____ ignore symptoms that are telling them a part of their body needs attention.

Help _____ listen to their whole physical being. If they are tired, help them rest; and give them sweet, regenerative sleep. If hungry, lead _____ to make wise choices of foods that are healthy with solid nutrition. If there are habits _____ needs to change: behavior, sleep, diet, exercise, then lead them to the conviction to make changes in those areas and give them the encouragement and strength that they need to follow through on whatever it takes to make those changes.

Thank You that You have created _____ body in such a miraculous way with redundancies and healing abilities within itself.

Even if there are serious or life-threatening issues, again be _____'s Healer. Command their body to line up with the way You created it to work. Bring _____ the discernment to know what to do, and when. If treatment is needed, give _____ courage to move forward with treatment, bringing medical teams who will be fully focused on their care with all their skill, talent, knowledge, experience and expertise to bear on _____'s case.

I acknowledge that _____'s life is Yours. Thank You for holding it so carefully in Your hands.

Let Good Health and Healing be a blessing from You, to _____ today. Amen

Reflections

How are you doing so far? If you have been able to be consistent in praying this week, good for you!

> If not, what has gotten in your way?
> How can you remedy that?

> You don't want to skip any blessings, so just pick up from where you left off.

During your prayer time this week, has God shown you anything about Himself?

_____

> About _____?

_____

> About yourself?

_____

In thinking back over the prayers prayed this week . . .

> Have you been able to see any blessings in _____'s life this week?

_____

> Can you identify a specific blessing they need now?

_____
> Ask God for that blessing for them now.

_____

Is there a blessing you prayed for them that you need to pray for yourself?

> Pray that prayer with your own name in the blanks now.

_____

Jot a Thank You here to God for anything you've seen that is a blessing from Him to you or the person you're praying for.

_____

_____

_____

Can you think of a time of difficulty or trouble, but God gave you a peace to deal with what you were facing? How did you sense that peace?

_____

_____

_____

If it's appropriate, consider how you might share that with the person you're praying for.

_____

There are so many ways God blesses us. Some people like to keep a Blessing Journal. You might make notes in this book about the blessings you experience during this 40-day journey.
Or you might get a notebook and look back on your life and jot down the times/circumstances when you felt blessed. Or just start from today forward.

Some people keep a bowl or basket on the table or a shelf and whenever they sense God has blessed them, they write it on a slip of paper. Then at the end of each week they read them and have a time of thanksgiving.

Recalling God's blessings to us is a great faith builder. Looking back on His faithfulness to you will help you trust in Him to be faithful in your future—whatever that may bring.

Psalm 89:1: *I will sing of the Lord's great love forever; with my mouth I will make your faithfulness known through all generations.*

A Sense of Your Presence

Psalm 16:11: *You make known to me the path of life; you will fill me with joy in your presence, with eternal pleasures at your right hand.*

Heavenly Father, open _____'s awareness to be able to sense Your presence with them. Let _____ feel You in real and tangible ways. And let them understand clearly that it is You, the One True God, Creator of the heavens and the earth, who is with them. And that they're not alone.

Let _____ feel close to You when they're in nature, like taking a walk or a hike. Or watching a sunset. Or listening to a stream. Or seeing birds fly overhead. Father give _____ that sense that there is something much bigger, more powerful, and creative, and good at work in the world and in their life.

When doing some physical activity or a chore, helping others, listening to music, or just relaxing... in their comings and their goings, in meetings and conversations, at work and in their home, with other people and when alone, let _____ have a sense of You being there with them.

If _____ is meditating, being quiet and reaching out to connect to some power, however they may search, protect that search so they find You. Quiet any other voices. Don't let _____ be fooled or enticed or misled by any other power. Father, let _____ connect with You.

Let that sense of Your presence be an amazing and wonderful comfort to _____ knowing that You've got their back, and they're protected. No matter what they're dealing with, let them know that *You can* handle it and that *You are willing* to handle it on their behalf.

Let Your presence also give _____ the courage to do what they know is right, to step out in the power that You bring. And strengthen them to be all that You created them to be; giving them the courage to move forward into the work that You have prepared in advance for them.

Let a sense of Your Presence be a blessing from You, to _____ today. Amen

Protection

Psalm 91:1-7: *Whoever dwells in the shelter of the Most High will rest in the shadow of the Almighty. I will say of the Lord, "He is my refuge and my fortress, my God, in whom I trust." Surely he will save you from the fowler's snare and from the deadly pestilence. He will cover you with his feathers, and under his wings you will find refuge; his faithfulness will be your shield and rampart. You will not fear the terror of night, nor the arrow that flies by day, nor the pestilence that stalks in the darkness, nor the plague that destroys at midday. A thousand may fall at your side, ten thousand at your right hand, but it will not come near you.*

Heavenly Father protect _____. Physically protect their life. Spread Your wings over them like a mother hen gathers her chicks. Protect them from danger, accident, illness, trauma, and violence. Protect their relationships, their home, their finances, their transportation, their job.

Watch over their comings and their goings. Protect their emotions and their spirit from any attack of the evil one, from any ungodly influence, and from the pressures of the world. And from their own flesh when their desires go against the good that You have in store for them.

Following the pattern of the scripture above Father, let _____ rest in Your shadow and find refuge under Your wings. Be their safe place in times of trouble. Save them from anyone who would ensnare them and from any deadly disease. By day and by night protect them from all attacks.

Do not let any harm overcome _____ or any disaster come near them. But command Your angels to guard them in all areas of their life. Let this protection lift them up so _____ will not fall or stumble, but be victorious, defeating their enemies. Rescue _____. Answer them in trouble. Deliver _____. And give them long life and salvation.

Let divine Protection be a blessing from You, to _____ today. Amen

The Solution to a Problem

Jeremiah 33:3: *Call to me and I will answer you and tell you great and unsearchable things you do not know.*

Heavenly Father I ask that You would supernaturally provide the solution to a problem or issue that _____ is facing. Whether at work or school, whether financial or with a relationship, whether facing a decision or an issue with their family or their home, I know You have the answer that will help them. Would You reveal that or lead _____ to that solution today.

Often, with the stress of facing difficult decisions or problems, we have a limited perspective and only see solutions that are right in front of us. Father, give _____ a greater perspective. Where they may only see choices A or B, open their eyes if You are presenting a totally new and unique answer. You can see options that are better solutions than anyone else could possibly think of or even imagine.

Father, move people, change circumstances, open doors that will show _____ that You are at work in their life to bring them answers to what concerns them. Delight _____ by presenting them with the solution they need in a way that they have no doubt it has come from You. And give them the courage to go forward with that solution.

Let a Solution to a Problem be a blessing from You to _____ today. Amen

Sleep

Psalm 4:8: *In peace I will lie down and sleep, for You alone, Lord, make me dwell in safety.*

Heavenly Father would You send _____ safe and sweet sleep that comes quickly and easily, without tossing and turning. Let _____'s sleep be regenerative and provide rest for their body and restoration for their soul. Provide sleep that will recharge their body with energy and healing. _____'s mind needs sleep to function well: to manage and organize the thoughts of the previous day and sort out new information, cataloging it into memory. Grant that.

Father, don't let stress and worry upset _____'s sleep habits. Falling asleep, help _____ let go of random or worrying thoughts and the stresses of the day. Let them sleep soundly through the night with no nightmares. Rather than having their sleep disturbed by activity in the house or neighborhood and waking up in that confusing state that leaves you mentally fuzzy and unable to focus on the day; allow _____ to wake up feeling rested and refreshed.

Help _____ listen to their body to get the sleep they need. Don't let them work to the point of physical or mental exhaustion. Help them recognize the signals: fuzzy thinking, inability to focus attention, irritability, silliness. Since how much sleep _____ needs changes with age, stress, health and other factors, give them wisdom for setting up their schedule with flexibility. Let them discern when something needs to be put off or delegated or simply not done. When tired and needing rest, don't let _____ fight it.

Bless _____ by letting them wake up feeling ready to face the day, energized, able to focus on all that lies ahead; feeling physically rested, mentally alert and emotionally clear. Maybe even waking up with the answer or solution to a problem they had before going to bed.

Let sweet Sleep be a blessing from You, to _____ today. Amen

Forgiveness

1 John 1:9: *If we confess our sins, he is faithful and just and will forgive us our sins and purify us from all unrighteousness.*

Heavenly Father, please prompt _____ to seek forgiveness and to forgive others.

Show _____ how to recognize sin in their life. Bring to mind sins that might be present in their thoughts, attitudes, speech, relationships, acts of rebellion against You, acts they have committed, or things they have failed to do that they know they should have done. Encourage _____ to confess any sin in their life to You.

Prod their heart and spirit with a conviction of that wrong, and a desire to turn from it. And lead _____ to ask for Your forgiveness.

As You grace them with Your forgiveness, and cleanse them from that sin, wash away any guilt or shame that has accompanied it. Tell _____ that when You forgive, You remove it from them as far as the east is from the west, and You remember their sin no more. And that when You cleanse them, they are made right and justified before You—"just as if" they'd never sinned.

Likewise, if _____ is harboring unforgiveness in their heart towards anyone else, help them forgive that offense. If something has happened in their life that caused pain by accident or misunderstanding, or even if it was caused through the evil intentions of another person, lead _____ by showing them how to forgive.

It's been said that unforgiveness is like drinking poison and expecting the other person to get sick or die. Don't let unforgiveness make _____ sick, bitter, and unhappy. Don't allow those past events to keep them chained to the offense and focused on vengeance, which You say belongs to You.

As _____ walks in the freedom of forgiveness, renew their spirit within them.

Let Forgiveness be a blessing from You, to _____ today. Amen

Heal broken places

Jeremiah 30:17a: *"But I will restore you to health and heal your wounds," declares the Lord.*

Heavenly Father, move into any places of brokenness _____ has in their life; those places where _____ is no longer strong physically, mentally, emotionally, or spiritually. It could be something related to their work, school, family, or relationships. Wherever there are broken places, speak Your life and Your healing. Give _____ faith to trust what You say: that You love them and that Your love is greater than whatever difficulty they're going through.

Heal those places where people have disappointed _____, or let them down, or even caused them pain. Meet _____'s emotional needs where relationships have been broken by betrayal, unmet expectations or dishonesty. Let them separate the pain of being hurt by fallible humans from their understanding of who You are. Encourage them to give You their life and their choices even through their brokenness.

These broken places are like weaknesses where _____ is vulnerable to temptation into sin and believing lies. Heal any spiritual wounds where they have believed lies and have kept You at a distance. While You are healing those areas, protect and encourage _____.

Protect them by hedging them in, in front and back, along their sides, above and below so that no evil power can get in and lead them farther away from You. Encourage _____ as You are healing them by bringing someone alongside them who will give wise counsel, and by checking their attitudes and guiding them into godly decisions.

Especially during these 40 days of prayer, be _____'s strength and spread Your protection over their body, mind and spirit. And heal their physical health and weaknesses. Thank You for being their Jehovah Rophe: their Healer.

Let the Healing of broken places be a blessing from You, to _____ today. Amen

Strength

Colossians 1:11: *Being strengthened with all power according to his glorious might.*

Heavenly Father, I thank You that our strength comes from You. I pray that You would strengthen _____ in whatever ways are needed for the circumstances they're experiencing today:

Strengthen _____ physically—for good health, stamina, energy, endurance to do the work before them or to enjoy recreational opportunities; for healing if there is an illness or injury, or a bolstering of _____'s immune system if exposed to any illness; for good rest and healthy eating; for easy breathing and the wisdom to not overdo it

Strengthen _____ mentally—for focus, to clear their mind of distracting thoughts as they make decisions, and the diligence to take every thought captive to You so they are not distracted by fears or the deceptive lies of the evil one, and to be alert to any dangers around them

Strengthen _____ emotionally—to deal with whatever decisions they face and the results of those decisions; to deal with anxiousness at circumstances beyond their control that affect _____ or their loved ones; relief from discouragement, sadness, fear, anger, guilt, depression, and the wisdom to get help from a godly counselor when necessary

Strengthen _____ spiritually—to have their faith bolstered by the remembrance that no matter what things may look like from an earthly perspective—You are in control. And give them spiritual strength to recognize and combat the enemy, dressed in Your spiritual armor

I ask that You would strengthen _____ with all power according to Your glorious might! Not mere human power where they try to do things in their own strength, but the power of the Living God acting in _____; so they may have great endurance and patience.

Let _____ live and walk in this strength and power to glorify You even in trials.

Let Strength be a blessing from You, to _____ today. Amen

Reflections

Two weeks—way to go! Are you finding a rhythm in your schedule for prayer?

_____

If you have been able to be consistent in praying this week—
Great Job!

    If not, what has gotten in your way?

    _____

    _____

    How can you remedy that?

    _____

    _____

    You don't want to skip any blessings, so just pick up from where you left off.

During your prayer time, what has God shown you about Himself?

_____

_____

_____

About _____?

_____

_____

About yourself?

_____

_____

In thinking back over the prayers prayed this week . . .

Have you been able to see any blessing in ____'s life this week?

_____

_____

Can you identify a specific blessing they need now?

_____

_____

Ask God for that blessing for them now.

_____

_____

Is there a blessing you prayed for them that you need to pray for yourself?

_____

_____

_____

Pray that prayer with your own name in the blanks now.

_____

_____

_____

_____

_____

Jot God a Thank You here for anything you've seen that is a blessing from Him to you or the person you're praying for.

_____

_____

_____

In what ways do you sense God's Presence?

_____

_____

Have you sensed it this week? How?

_____

_____

_____

Would sharing any of these with the person you're praying for help them recognize God at work in their own life?

_____

If it's appropriate, consider how you might share these with the person you're praying for.

_____

_____

In praying about forgiveness, did anyone come to mind who you need to forgive?

_____

If so, ask God what steps you need to take in order to do that.

_____

_____

Did anything come to mind you need to seek forgiveness for?

_____

_____

If so, set aside time to confess to God and ask forgiveness

_____

Do you still have broken places in your own life that need God's healing touch?

_____

If you aren't sure, ask God to show you if there are places where you are vulnerable to temptation. Or where your emotions rise up unexpectedly.

_____

_____

_____

Set aside some time this week to get alone with God and pour out your heart to Him. Show Him where there is hurt from the past. Ask for God to move in your life with whatever is needed for your personal healing.

Even if you don't have broken places, set aside some time to be alone with God and share whatever is on your heart—what you've been doing—this 40-day journey—your challenges—your hopes and dreams.

List what you might share with Him here:

_____

_____

_____

_____

Hear Your Voice

Isaiah 30:21: *Whether you turn to the right or to the left, your ears will hear a voice behind you, saying, "This is the way; walk in it."*

Heavenly Father help _____ learn how to recognize Your voice from all the other voices they hear in the world and in their own minds. Show them how to:

1. Tune in to the ways You speak to them
2. Tune out the distracting voices around and inside them
3. Clean out any "ear infection" of sin

Like the sheep know the voice of their Shepherd let _____ become familiar with and "tune in" to the sound of Your voice and be responsive to what You have to say to them. And open their spiritual ears to hear all You would say regarding their life, their circumstances, relationships, business and personal decisions, their purpose, and Your amazing, unconditional love for them.

Obviously, You speak through Your Word, the Holy Spirit, and in prayer when we listen. Remind _____ to seek out those ways to hear You. Father, reach them in dreams, revelations and visions; through Your creation, their circumstances, and through blessings. Let them hear Your voice through other mature Christians speaking in books, podcasts, and from the pulpit, and through doors that You open. But help _____ also understand that You speak through the doors that You close, through pain, through people who rub them the wrong way too. Open _____'s spiritual ears to what You would have to say to them through any of these and help them understand You clearly.

At the same time show _____ how to tune out the world, which is competing for their attention, telling them what they should do, wear, eat, and buy; overwhelming them with messages. Even the inner voices they hear are so often negative and critical. Father, silence those voices for _____ so they can hear Your voice the loudest.

Sin can be like an "ear infection" that prevents us from hearing You clearly. Make _____ aware of any sin in their life. Prompt them to confess those to You for forgiveness. And then to wait to hear from You.

Answer them quickly so they will not be left in confusion.

Let Hearing Your Voice be a blessing from You, to _____ today. Amen

Love

Ephesians 3:17-19: *And I pray that you...may have power... to grasp how wide and long and high and deep is the love of Christ, and to know this love that surpasses knowledge.*

Heavenly Father, You so loved _____ that You made the ultimate sacrifice for them to have a relationship with You for all eternity. Help _____ "know" of Your unconditional love for the entire world, but also for them personally.

Heavenly Father, pour out Your extraordinary, supernatural love on _____ in ways they can sense and recognize are coming from You. Let them feel the breadth and the length, the height and the depth of Your love for them as Your child, personally. And let it have an amazing and profound effect on them.

We don't always perceive the love that others have for us by the ways they show it. But Father, You speak every love language. Speak to _____ of Your love in the language You created them to receive it. Your love is complete, unconditional, and extravagant! Lavish that love, attention and care on _____ in a way they can see it comes from You.

The evil one would try to tell us we do not deserve Your love. And we don't. That we have let You down so have not earned Your love. And we haven't. We never can. But do not let _____ be swayed by these attacks from the evil one. In truth, You love because You are love. And You love _____, because they are Your creation!

Even if _____ feels unlovable, You still love them. _____ is the apple of Your eye. If you had one, _____'s picture would be on Your refrigerator or in Your cell phone :). Help them "feel" it and understand what it means to be loved by You. Give them the ability to understand Your love, and to live and walk in it.

Let Your Love be a blessing from You, to _____ today. Amen

Time Management

Ephesians 5:15–16: *Look carefully then how you walk, not as unwise, but as wise, making the best use of the time... (ESV)*

Heavenly Father, please help _____ use their time and energy wisely. Even with the same number of minutes and hours in each day, some seem to pass by so quickly and we feel like we haven't gotten the important things done. And other days seem much more productive. Help _____ be productive in their use of focus and energy in the time they have each day.

Father, multiply _____'s time. Help them work smarter, not harder. Let them see when tasks can be combined to save energy and running around. Show them how to accomplish tasks quickly and efficiently even when there are interruptions.

Help _____ distinguish between what is important and what is urgent, and not confuse the two. Show them how to structure their days to make time for those things that are important, even if they're not urgent. And give them discernment to know when an interruption is just a distraction, and when it is from You, to be attended to.

Help _____ see where balance is needed for appropriate amounts of time to focus on work, rest, relationships, and leisure time. Multiply _____'s energy and strength to do what is needed on a daily basis to deal with their circumstances.

Don't let _____ believe the lie that "I work better under pressure." Or feel like they have to do everything themselves when some things are done better by someone else, or can be delegated or hired out. One of the devil's strategies is to invite us to do things that consume our enthusiasm, time, and energy so we don't get around to doing what You have called us to do. Father, do not let _____'s schedule be so busy they don't have time to hear from You.

Let good Time Management be a blessing from You to _____ today. Amen

Direction

Psalm 32:8: *I will instruct you and teach you in the way you should go; I will counsel you with my loving eye on you.*

Heavenly Father, guide _____ in and through the circumstances of their life. In good times let them rejoice and be thankful. In troubled times draw them close to You for comfort, support, and focus. Show _____ how to learn from mistakes and be reassured that You don't waste anything, but are in the business of reconciliation and redemption.

You rarely show us a map of how our entire life will go, but You can show _____ steps to take now from where they are. Give _____ enough of a glimpse into their future to know what direction to head and how You will use the gifts and talents You've placed in them.

Regarding the circumstances in _____'s life around work and career, finances, relationships, health, family, travel—help them count the cost and see the risks and benefits clearly from Your viewpoint. Keep _____ from running headlong into decisions based only on what they think they see with their physical eyes or understand from their perspective.

Show _____ how to set godly priorities. Help them take the time to recognize what is important and what is not. Not just what seems urgent at the time.

Let _____ hear Your wise counsel and understand how You are directing them. If a decision needs to be made, teach _____ how to ask You in prayer and listen for Your answer. You speak in so many ways, give _____ a clear understanding of Your direction. And confirm it with scripture or a word from a wise Christian in their life.

Show them where You are at work opening or closing a door with finances, career, relationships, family, health, ministry, and needs in every area of their life. And how to be bold to walk through those doors You open, and honor those doors You close.

When _____ has confirmation of the direction You would lead, help them "Be strong and courageous . . . not afraid . . . or discouraged . . . " for You will be with them wherever they go (Joshua 1:9).

Let godly Direction be a blessing from You to _____ today. Amen

Encouragement

Isaiah 41:10: *So do not fear, for I am with you; do not be dismayed, for I am your God. I will strengthen you and help you; I will uphold you with my righteous right hand.*

Heavenly Father, so many events in our lives cause us to feel discouraged emotionally and spiritually. Please bring the emotional and spiritual encouragement and support that _____ needs to deal with the challenges and trials they face daily, as well as the more difficult burdens that arise.

Fill _____ with the motivation and courage they need to meet whatever lies before them in order to be bolstered up, energized to go on mentally, emotionally and spiritually. You created _____. And You knew beforehand the purpose of their life, the places they would go, and the perils they would face. You carefully fashioned _____ and have prepared them to handle, with Your help, whatever they need to face now. Show them how You have already built into them the confidence, the faith, and the tools they need.

Bring whatever _____ needs in the moment—the solution to a problem, a new perspective, another person to help with the load, a word from a friend, a stranger's smile, a beautiful sunset. Let _____ hear truth from Your Word, or recall scriptures that reinforce Your love and support for them. And show them how to insert their name to make Your promises personal. Like this:

_____ will not fear, for You, Lord, are with them; _____ will not be dismayed for You are their God. You will strengthen _____ and help them, You will uphold _____ with Your righteous right hand (Isaiah 41:10).

You are with _____ always. You will always be holding their hand; You will guide _____ with Your counsel, and take them into glory...You are the strength of _____'s heart and their portion forever (Psalm 73:23-26).

Help _____ recognize how You are at work in their life, or how, in the past, You were faithful to them. And let the memory of those times strengthen and build their faith, trusting You will be there for them now. Let _____ observe courage in others facing similar challenges and learn from their mistakes and triumphs.

Even as _____ knows they need to do their part, let them rest assured that You will do Your part.

Let Encouragement be a blessing from You to _____ today. Amen

Hope

Jeremiah 29:11: *For I know the plans I have for you," declares the Lord, "plans to prosper you and not to harm you, plans to give you a hope and a future.*

Heavenly Father, I pray that whatever _____ is facing in their life right now, that You would give them hope.

Not the kind of hope that's just wishful thinking like, "I hope I win the lottery." But a hope that is based on faith in You - that You have good things planned for _____ because You love them. And a hope that no matter what the world or anyone else can throw at them, You are the most powerful force in the universe, and have the ability to thwart the plans of rulers and kings and any other power on the planet!

Father, fight against any thought, emotion or power that causes _____ to feel so overwhelmed as to believe there is no solution to whatever they're dealing with. Do not let _____ ever feel that life is so out of control that it is hopeless. Regardless of their circumstances, do not let them entertain any thoughts of harming themself. Because sometimes giving up may seem the easy way out, let Your hope shine a light on their next step. And provide _____ with the motivation and courage to take any step You show them, even if it's difficult.

Let Your hope fill _____ with joy and a peace that passes all understanding by the power of the Holy Spirit. Let it give them a new, godly perspective on their circumstances. Fill _____ with the knowledge that they are not alone. And that whatever the issue, whatever the problem, and whatever the difficulty they face, You have the power and the desire to help them. And that You can do immeasurably more than they can ask or even imagine.

Let Hope be a blessing from You to _____ today. Amen

Be their Shepherd

Psalm 23: *The LORD is my shepherd, I lack nothing.*
He makes me lie down in green pastures,
he leads me beside quiet waters, he refreshes my soul.
He guides me along the right paths for his name's sake.
Even though I walk through the darkest valley, I will fear no evil,
for you are with me; your rod and your staff, they comfort me.
You prepare a table before me in the presence of my enemies.
You anoint my head with oil; my cup overflows.
Surely your goodness and love will follow me all the days of my
life, and I will dwell in the house of the LORD forever.

Heavenly Father, You are the Good Shepherd. _____ is Your sheep. Please show special care for this sheep. Attend to their personal needs as a good shepherd would so they want for nothing. Remind them to take time to rest and lie down in the green pastures You have prepared for them.

If _____ has become entangled in the thorny briars of this world, or has wandered away, guide them with Your staff into Your paths of righteousness and calm waters to drink from, and away from swift-moving deep waters that can drown them.

If _____ feels as if they are walking in the shadow of death, be with them. Comfort and protect them. Lend _____ Your courage to face whatever is before them, even in the presence of their enemy. Restore their soul as only You can.

Give _____ a strong sense of being in Your flock living in safety under Your tender care. And the remembrance that they are Your sheep forever.

Let the awareness of being a sheep of The Good Shepherd be a blessing from You to _____ today. Amen

Reflections

You are more than halfway through this 40-day journey!
AWESOME! We are cheering you on!!

If you have been able to be consistent in praying this week,
good for you!

If not, what has gotten in your way?

_____

How can you remedy that?

_____

You don't want to skip any blessings, so just pick up from
where you left off.

During your prayer time, what has God shown you about Himself?

_____

About ____?

_____

About yourself?

_____

_____

In thinking back over the prayers prayed this week...

Can you identify a specific blessing _____ needs now?

_____

Ask God for that blessing for them now.

Is there a blessing you prayed for them that you need to pray for yourself?

_____

Pray that prayer with your own name in the blanks now.

_____

Jot God a Thank You here for anything you've seen that is a blessing from Him to you or the person you're praying for.

_____

What are the ways you hear from God?

_____

How do you "tune in" to God's voice and "tune out" other distractions?

_____

How do you confirm it's God speaking to you?

_____

Check out the Hearing God Guide and Worksheet in the Appendix at the back of this book. Page 116

Is there a time in your life when you received direction, encouragement or hope from God?

What did it look like?

_____

Would sharing any of these with the person you're praying for help them recognize God at work in their own life?

If it's appropriate, consider how you might share these with the person you're praying for.

Half way point check:

Have you sensed any pushback?

_____

When you pray for another person, sometimes the blowback comes on you and you can find yourself facing hardship or discouragement yourself. It could be an upset with the one you're praying for—or any other relationship, or your work or home life. Maybe a sudden health issue or unexplained crisis. It may seem to come out of the blue, with no warning and no logic as to why things are happening. Praying for someone else does not make the evil one happy.

Have you experienced anything like that? What?

_____

_____

If this happens it's helpful to be sure you are praying on armor of God as part of your daily prayer time. Even a simple prayer like:

> _Heavenly Father, thank You for the armor You give me that protects me as I pray. I put on the Helmet of Salvation to protect my mind, and the Breastplate of Righteousness to protect my chest and organs. I put on the Belt of Truth to help me discern truth and reject any lies. I wear the Shoes of the Gospel of Peace and take up the Shield of Faith and the sword of the Spirit to fight in the battles You call me to._

For more information see the Resource Guide on Spiritual Armor for Battle in the Appendix at the back of the book. Pages 111–113

And pray for yourself, asking God to guard you and protect you, your family, your health, finances, relationships, home, job, and whatever else you feel led to pray about in your life that could be under attack. Ask God to keep you standing firm.

_____

_____

_____

_____

It also helps to talk with another Christian friend and ask them to pray for you and what you're experiencing. Or even for the duration of this 40-day journey.

Deliverance

2 Corinthians 1:10: *He has delivered us from such a deadly peril, and he will deliver us again. On him we have set our hope that he will continue to deliver us . . .*

Heavenly Father deliver _____ from influences they do not understand or that are too great for them, or that would lead them away from You. Loosen the hold the world has on them or that the evil one would seek to gain. If they do not recognize it, if there is any ungodly or occult influence in their home or life, reveal it to _____.

If _____ has sought anything to be a comfort, a distraction, or any behavior or substance that has become an addiction, open their eyes to the problem. Convict their spirit of what needs to change. Do not let them be afraid or discouraged, but see Your hand in delivering them.

Loosen their grip on anything _____ has put above You, and return them to Your counsel. If they have gotten themselves into situations that have manipulated or overpowered them, remove them from the hold of those powers that seek to destroy them and pull them away from You.

If _____ has been bound or chained with any addiction, idol worship, or some other power affecting their life, Father break those chains. If there is some behavior they've been trying to control or stop, remove the desire and the urgency to continue in it.

Father, give _____ an immediate victory, delivering them from the grasp of idolatry or sin or evil.

Let Deliverance be a blessing from You, to _____ today. Amen

Family

2 Corinthians 13:11: *Strive for full restoration, encourage one another, be of one mind, live in peace. And the God of love and peace will be with you.*

Heavenly Father, it is Your plan that family be a source of support and strength and joy. Sometimes the family we have here on earth is loving and kind and supportive. If that is the case for _____, help them realize what they have and give You thanks. Even the best family is only made up of people though, and people are imperfect. And it seems those we are closest to have the ability to frustrate and wound us the most.

But some family relationships are far from loving, kind and supportive. Instead they are the source of fighting, manipulation, even abuse. Father, help _____ cope with the family situations they face. Protect them from abuse, manipulation and deception. When necessary, help _____ gain the physical or emotional distance from those who are hurting them or leading them away from You.

Where reconciliation is possible, let _____ be willing to restore positive relationships. Provide opportunities to build bridges and work out differences. Where personal decisions affect family relationships, show _____ how to be open and honest about their needs and concerns, and those of the family. Remind them to make time to seek Your wisdom and perspective.

Bring people into _____'s life who will be the support they need, people who they can lean on, who will give them godly advice and encouragement, and pray for them. Let these people build healthy relationships with _____ and be like family to them.

Let healthy Family relationships be a blessing from You to _____ today. Amen

Knowledge

Psalm 119:66: *Teach me knowledge and good judgment, for I trust your commands.*

Heavenly Father, give _____ knowledge about who You are, about who they are, and about the world around them. Help them see the truth in the knowledge that the Bible gives. Show them a real view of the world and how it works. Expose any lies or deceiving beliefs or philosophies that have led them away from Your truth.

In their personal life, bring access to up-to-date and accurate knowledge that _____ needs for their circumstances right now. Bring that information to light in a timely manner so they can make wise decisions based on all the evidence. Don't let them be misled by a lack of or incorrect information.

If a decision needs to be made and there is information that would affect the outcome, draw their attention to it. Where information isn't forthcoming, help _____ know the questions to ask that will reveal what they need to know. If anything is hidden, I ask for transparency and sharing in good faith from anyone who has the knowledge. Father, shine Your light on what _____ needs to know.

If a relationship is suffering from misinformation or misunderstanding, allow clarification, and bring what needs to be known out into the open.

Father, don't let _____ be deceived by inaccurate, untimely or plain false communications. So many details affect our lives and the decisions we make. Reveal what needs to be known so _____ can be wise in their job, in their relationships, in finances, in health decisions, in life decisions they're facing.

Let Knowledge be a blessing from You to _____ today. Amen

Humor

Proverbs 17:22: *A cheerful heart is good medicine, but a crushed spirit dries up the bones.*

Heavenly Father, would You help _____ find joy and humor around them today and every day. Proverbs tells us that laughter is good medicine for the soul. And a happy heart makes a cheerful countenance. Let them present a happy heart to the world

When things are going well, remind _____ to smile and spread joy to others. You tell us to rejoice always! So instead of looking for trouble, let their heart be light. When dealing with both the expected and the unexpected, let _____ not be anxious, but bring everything to You in prayer. And then leave their concerns in Your capable hands.

Don't allow the stress of any challenge to overtake _____'s focus or cloud their mind. When needed, whether it's just been a long hard day or something difficult or troubling has just happened, remind them to take a "Laugh Break!" For instance, they could read the comics, watch a funny movie, tell a joke, and invite people around them who make them laugh. Show _____ how to release tension, whether it's for an afternoon, an hour, or just cracking a joke or two.

What did the man say when all his lamps were stolen? I'm de-lighted!

Father, let a good sense of humor lift _____'s spirit and lighten their burden. Even in times of challenge or trouble, help them be able to laugh and smile. Rekindle their sense of humor and wonder at the world. Let laughter be a balm for their soul.

Job 8:21 says, "He will once again fill your mouth with laughter and your lips with shouts of joy." Fill _____ with Your laughter and Your joy.

Let Humor be a blessing from You to _____ today. Amen

Patient Endurance

Colossians 1:11: *. . . being strengthened with all power according to his glorious might so that you may have great endurance and patience.*

Heavenly Father, give _____ patient endurance. If they are facing something now that is not happening for them — or at least not happening in the amount of time they had hoped it would, show them how to wait and endure; to hold on until it does happen. Or until You show them something better.

Endurance often means that someone needs to bear up under the pressure of something arduous and difficult, longer than they think they are able. Father, strengthen _____ to be able to bear it and give them the stamina they need to outlast the challenge they're facing.

Other times it means waiting on something to begin. Enduring a delay can be just as trying. Give _____ what they need to deal with postponements or changes.

Try as we might, we cannot simply make ourselves be more patient. But You can help _____ learn how to wait purposefully, prayerfully and praise-fully. Reveal to them that there is a purpose in Your timing, that You are in control, and that Your timing is perfect, bringing blessing. Give _____ something to be doing as they wait that has meaning while they can't be moving forward with the specific thing they are waiting on.

During the waiting time, let their thoughts, plans, even frustrations trigger prayer. Encourage _____ to bring all those concerns to You. And as they talk it out and listen to Your answers, they will learn patience. Let it also be a time of praising You for who You are, for all You've done, and for all You will do as You continue to be at work in their life.

Let Patient Endurance be a blessing from You to _____ today. Amen

Spiritual Protection

Ephesians 6:12: *For our struggle is not against flesh and blood, but against the rulers, against the authorities, against the powers of this dark world and against the spiritual forces of evil in the heavenly realms.*

Heavenly Father protect and guide _____ in their comings and goings. Do not let _____ seek after evil or be tempted by the temporary pleasures of evil. But let them see and seek what is good and right and just.

Let them have experiences that bear out Your truth about what is overtly evil and what is actually good. Even let _____ learn from the painful lessons and experiences of others that evil does not pay, and that it will cost them more than they anticipate.

I am aware there are spiritual enemies who seek to undermine _____'s faith and ability to do the work You created them to do. So I put their name into Psalm 35 and pray Your words against the rulers, against the authorities, and against the spiritual powers of this dark world, and the spiritual forces in the heavenly realms who set themselves up against You and Your will for _____ to protect their life, health, family, relationships, home, school or work, finances, mental and emotional well-being and spiritual growth.

Psalm 35 Of David.

[1] Contend, Lord, with those who contend with [_____];
    fight against those who fight against [them].
[2] Take up shield and armor;
    arise and come to [their] aid.
[3] Brandish spear and javelin
    against those who pursue [_____].
Say to [_____],
    "I am your salvation."
[4] May those who seek [_____'s] life
    be disgraced and put to shame;
may those who plot [their] ruin

be turned back in dismay.
5 May they be like chaff before the wind,
   with the angel of the Lord driving them away;
6 may their path be dark and slippery,
   with the angel of the Lord pursuing them.
7 Since they hid their net for [_____] without cause
   and without cause dug a pit for [them],
8 may ruin overtake them by surprise—
   may the net they hid entangle them,
   may they fall into the pit, to their ruin.
9 Then my soul will rejoice in the Lord
   and delight in His salvation.
10 My whole being will exclaim,
   "Who is like you, Lord?
You rescue the poor [_____] from those too strong for them,
   the poor and needy [_____] from those who rob them."
11 Ruthless witnesses come forward;
   they question [_____] on things [they] know nothing about.
12 They repay [_____] evil for good
   and leave [them] like one bereaved.
15 But when [_____] stumbled, they gathered in glee;
   assailants gathered against [_____] without [their] knowledge.
   They slandered [them] without ceasing.
16 Like the ungodly they maliciously mocked;
   they gnashed their teeth at [_____].
17 How long, Lord, will you look on?
   Rescue [_____] from their ravages,
   [their] precious life from these lions.
18 I will give you thanks in the great assembly;
   among the throngs I will praise you.

¹⁹ Do not let those gloat over [_____]
    who are [their] enemies without cause;
do not let those who hate [_____] without reason
    maliciously wink the eye.
²⁰ They do not speak peaceably,
    but devise false accusations
    against those who live quietly in the land.
²¹ They sneer at [_____] and say, "Aha! Aha!
    With our own eyes we have seen it."
²² LORD, you have seen this; do not be silent.
    Do not be far from [_____], Lord.
²³ Awake, and rise to [_____'s] defense!
    Contend for [them], my God and Lord.
²⁴ Vindicate [_____] in your righteousness, LORD my God;
    do not let them gloat over [_____].
²⁵ Do not let them think, "Aha, just what we wanted!"
    or say, "We have swallowed [them] up."
²⁶ May all who gloat over [_____'s] distress
    be put to shame and confusion;
may all who exalt themselves over [_____]
    be clothed with shame and disgrace.
²⁷ May those who delight in [_____'s] vindication
    shout for joy and gladness;
may they always say, "The LORD be exalted,
    who delights in the well-being of his servant."
²⁸ My tongue will proclaim Your righteousness,
    Your praises all day long.

Let Your Spiritual Protection be a blessing from You, to _____ today. Amen

Divine Appointments

Philippians 2:13: *For it is God who works in you to will and to act in order to fulfill his good purpose.*

Heavenly Father, give _____ "Divine Appointments" in their life. Arrange opportunities for them to be in the right place at the right time to hear or see something or someone who will contribute to understanding Your love for _____, and Your provision for their life.

Orchestrate meetings with other people who can introduce them to the answers they're looking for. Lead them to people who exemplify godly behavior, language and character and can be a blessing in _____'s life.

Whether these will become lifelong friendships, or just be a momentary influence in _____'s life, let these happenings occur often. Create a constant stream of positive, godly and encouraging direction for _____.

Heavenly Father, You created the universe! Let _____ witness events or casual occurrences that make a connection with You and Your power. Help _____ discover You in a podcast, or the theme of a movie or a real-life discussion. Let them see You in a joy or challenge they experience. When these Divine Appointments happen, don't let _____ miss the significance of what is occurring. Open their mind and heart and spirit to the influences You bring their way.

Let Divine Appointments be a blessing from You to _____. Amen

Reflections

Amazing job! You have completed Day 28! Way to go!!

If you have not been able to be consistent in praying this week, what has gotten in your way? And how can you remedy that?

_____

_____

You don't want to skip any blessings, so just pick up from where you left off.

During your prayer time, what has God shown you about Himself?

_____

_____

About _____?

_____

_____

About yourself?

_____

_____

In thinking back over the prayers prayed this week...

     Have you been able to see any blessing in _____'s life this week?

     _____

     Can you identify a specific blessing they need now?

     _____

     Ask God for that blessing for them now.

Is there a blessing you prayed for them that you need to pray for yourself?

_____

Pray that prayer with your own name in the blanks now.

_____

_____

Jot God a Thank You here for anything you've seen that is a blessing from Him to you or the person you're praying for.

_____

_____

When was the last time you felt God gave you the patience or endurance you needed to deal with a difficult situation?

_____

Is there a time you experienced God's deliverance or spiritual protection in some way? What was that like?

_____

_____

Have you had any Divine Appointments? Something that just happened to work out where you felt God must have orchestrated it?

_____

_____

How did they come about?

_____

_____

If it's appropriate, consider how you might share these with the person you're praying for.

Mercy and Grace

2 Samuel 24:14: *Let us fall into the hands of the* L<small>ORD</small>*, for his mercy is great.*

2 Thessalonians 2:16: *. . . our Lord Jesus Christ himself and God our Father, who loved us and by his grace gave us eternal encouragement and good hope*

Mercy is withholding something actually deserved like a punishment or a consequence. Grace is giving what is not earned.

Heavenly Father, show _____ where You have extended them mercy. Let them grasp all the times You have shown them mercy, understanding it was not just "luck" that brought them favor. And let _____ see that out of Your great love for them, You are granting them mercy again in the circumstances of their lives now.

Remind _____ that mercy is not something they can earn or that they deserve, but it is a free gift from You. And make them aware of those in their life right now who need mercy from them. Embolden _____ to withhold judgment and extend mercy where they would even have a right to do otherwise. And in so doing, become a blessing to others.

Reassure _____ that You have already equipped them with resources, abilities, and everything they need to accomplish the work that You have prepared in advance for them. Paul tells the Philippians that it is God who works in us to fulfill His good purposes. And there may be many good purposes and invitations to join You in those works throughout _____'s lifetime.

Heavenly Father show _____ where You have extended them grace throughout their lives. Let them see where, by Your favor and out of Your love, You have blessed them with benefits they could not have earned or did not deserve. But that out of Your never changing character and abundant grace You've blessed them.

Give _____ Your grace now; Your unmerited favor with whatever issue they are dealing with and let them see that without a doubt it has come from You. In their relationships, their work, personal circumstances, be merciful and gracious. Let them receive wisdom and favor in their families, at their job, making decisions, and in difficult circumstances. And in turn, be merciful and gracious to others.

Let giving and receiving Mercy and Grace be a blessing from You to _____ today. Amen

Clear Communication

Zechariah 8:16: *These are the things you are to do: Speak the truth to each other and render true and sound judgment in your courts.*

Heavenly Father, please bless _____ with clear communication with family, loved ones, and people they work or serve with. Bless their conversations with openness and honesty without lies, deception or innuendo playing a part. Give _____ clarity, without assumptions having to be made, or having to try and guess what is meant by what is or isn't said.

If there are business, financial, or personal decisions to be made, allow for interactions to be completely transparent. See that all negotiations are done in good faith, with accurate information, openly conveyed honestly and correctly. If questions need to be asked in order to clarify or reveal something not shared, then give _____ the questions to ask.

Especially with important relationships, let there be no trying to cover up hurt feelings, no intentionally misleading statements, but let people say what they mean and mean what they say.

If there is any falseness or misinformation shared for any reason, make _____ aware of it. And guide them in what to say or do to get to the truth of the issue.

Family communication can be the hardest. It is so easy to keep an account of wrong or hurtful things said. And there is often emotion tied to our words that can wound deeply. To keep the peace, we may even hold things in that fester and grow out of proportion if not dealt with. Father, help _____ by orchestrating the time and circumstances to allow for grievances to be aired in an open and healthy way so that no root of bitterness grows.

Let Clear Communication be a blessing from You to _____ today. Amen

Calling

Ephesians 2:10: *For we are God's handiwork, created in Christ Jesus to do good works, which God prepared in advance for us to do.*

Heavenly Father, give _____ a sense of the work You have created them for and prepared for them to do. Give them an understanding of how You created them; with specific gifts, talents, and personality; and how You would use those to accomplish Your will through their life.

Father, You are already at work in the world in countless ways. Open _____'s eyes and heart to opportunities that arise where You are inviting them to join You. It might be a career, a temporary job, a ministry or volunteer position. Or some way You would use a hobby or interest or skill _____ has that will bless someone else.

You might invite _____ to go around the block or around the world. Help them understand how You have uniquely created them- their personality, spiritual gifts, talents, abilities, and passions, to help others, and change and impact lives for the better. And how using those gifts and talents will bring _____ a sense of accomplishment, satisfaction and joy.

Reassure _____ that You have already equipped them with resources, abilities, and everything they need to accomplish the work that You have prepared in advance for them. Paul tells the Philippians that it is God who works in us to fulfill His good purposes. And there may be many good purposes and invitations to join You in those works throughout _____'s lifetime.

Whether _____ is looking for a vocational job, a place in ministry or volunteer work, or making other decisions about their future, open doors and close doors that will or will not benefit them. Do not let _____ be led astray by the world or anyone else who would seek to manipulate or control them with these choices.

Lead _____ to a position or place that will recognize and use the talents and abilities You have gifted them with. Shed enough light for _____ to see and take the next step. Speak in their ear and tell them "This is the way, walk in it" (Isaiah 20:31).

Let a Calling be a blessing from You to _____ today. Amen

Role Models/Mentor

2 Timothy 3:14: *. . . continue in what you have learned and have become convinced of, because you know those from whom you learned it.*

Heavenly Father, please send godly role models into _____'s life. Bring people who will speak Your truth and model how to live that truth in this ungodly world. You know the kind of person that can impact and influence _____. Send someone they will respect and listen to into their sphere of contact who will make an impression on them.

Open _____'s eyes and ears to the presence of these role models. Create opportunities for them to interact. Let these good examples illustrate how they're choosing to live their life and make wise decisions. Even let _____ learn from the mistakes others have made in the past so they don't have to make the same mistakes.

And in addition to role models, bring a mentor to _____ who will take an active interest in them and in their spiritual development. It may be someone they already know. Or it could be a brand-new contact who they can make a connection with.

Father, provide opportunities for this mentor to observe and speak into _____'s life on all kinds of issues: relational, professional, financial, social and spiritual. Give them Your wisdom to know how to interact with and be involved with _____ in a natural, relaxed way.

Thank You that You use ordinary people in all our lives for extraordinary purposes.

Let godly Role Models and Mentors be a blessing from You to _____ today. Amen

Courage

Joshua 1:5–6: *No one will be able to stand against you all the days of your life. As I was with Moses, so I will be with you; I will never leave you nor forsake you. Be strong and courageous.*

Heavenly Father would You give _____ the courage they need to move forward in their life.

Make them bold enough to step out when You call them to something. Strengthen _____'s resolve to do what they believe You are directing them to do, whether it's in a professional arena of their work, ministry, or on a personal level. Clarify the what, why and how of the situation and give them confidence in how You have prepared them with their identity, their character, their talent, their abilities, and their motivation.

Reassure _____ that whatever You have chosen them to do You will equip them to do. That what You have ordained, You will sustain. If there are choices to be made, give _____ discernment to see the right way to go. And if there is no right or wrong then help them in their freedom of choice. Strengthen their mental, emotional, and spiritual boldness.

Reassure them with a sense of Your presence. Remind them You have promised to be with them and never leave them. If something is holding them back, let _____ know that You have overcome the world, and that Your victory is theirs. If they face an enemy, keep their focus on You, who are bigger than any enemy, so they will not fear.

Bring others around _____ who will give them the encouragement and support they need: physically, emotionally, financially, and spiritually. And silence every voice that is not from You or that would keep them from doing what You are leading them to.

Let Courage be a blessing from You to _____ today. Amen

Known and Accepted

Isaiah 43:1: *But now, this is what the LORD says — he who created you, Jacob, he who formed you, Israel: 'Do not fear, for I have redeemed you; I have summoned you by name; you are mine.*

Heavenly Father, most of our lives we seek to be known and accepted. Help _____ overcome any thoughts of rejection by being assured that You, the Creator of the universe, know them completely, and accept them as they are.

The voices of the world, the evil one, and even our own thoughts so often turn to criticism and judgment, and crush our spirit. Remind _____ that You created them uniquely, fearfully and wonderfully (Psalm 139). That before they were born, You knew them and had a wonderful purpose and plan for them (Jeremiah 1:5 and 29:11).

Show _____ how to have confidence in their strengths and weaknesses, trusting that You artfully and skillfully created them and are satisfied with who they are. Challenge _____ to use their strengths to honor You and to allow their weaknesses to draw them closer to You so Your strength will show through them.

Assure _____ that their life is not some radical self-improvement course, but that because You love them, You are at work in their life. _____ is Your child, forever. You have said neither life nor death, neither angels nor demons, nor anything else in creation can separate _____ from Your love for them (Romans 8:38-39). And _____ is precious and honored in Your sight (Isaiah 43:4).

Let the assurance of being Known and Accepted by You be a blessing from You to _____ today. Amen

Joy

Ps 105:43: *He brought out his people with rejoicing, his chosen ones with shouts of joy.*

Heavenly Father, please give _____ a sense of true joy today. I don't mean something that might bring them simple happiness or a temporary pleasure as judged by the world's standards. So, not just fame or fortune, or what the world would call success. Because You can do far more than I could ever ask or even imagine, I'm not even sure what that would look like in their life.

Father, You know _____ best. You know the desires of their heart. You know the depth of their soul. Bless them with a gift that will fill their soul with deep joy, a sense of sincere and honest satisfaction that brings a smile to their face and peace to their heart.

It could be something _____ has been planning, or hoping for, for a long time that You finally bring. Or it could be something they don't even expect that takes them totally by surprise. You can give joy in the midst of suffering and pain. You can fill the heart that was weeping with rejoicing. You are capable of wonders beyond human imagination. You can do miracles!

Father, let this joy be a source of strength for _____, to carry them through times of stress or challenge. Let it be a source of light when there is darkness around them.

Let true Joy be a blessing from You to _____ today. Amen

Reflections

You are almost there!! Great job!! We are so proud of you!

If you have missed any days don't skip those blessings, just pick up from where you left off.

During your prayer time, what has God shown you about Himself?

_____

About _____?

_____

About yourself?

_____

In thinking back over the prayers prayed this week...

Have you been able to see any blessing in your person's life this week?

_____

Can you identify a specific blessing they need now?

_____

Ask God for that blessing for them now.

_____

Is there a blessing you prayed for them that you need to pray for yourself?

_____

Pray that prayer with your own name in the blanks now.

_____

Jot God a Thank You here for anything you've seen that is a blessing from Him to you or the person you're praying for.

_____

When was the last time you felt God directed or invited you to use your gifts and talents for a specific purpose?

_____

    Did you accept? What happened?

    _____

    Do you sense there might be another invitation for you to respond to now?

    _____

There are many resources for you to discover your specific uniqueness. Consider investigating some time to discover your spiritual gifts, your personality strengths, your abilities and experiences, and what you have a heart for or are passionate about. I believe God wants you to delight in using your strengths and talents and will invite you to join Him in areas you would enjoy where He is already at work.

Do you have a role model or mentor in your life? Or are you a role model or mentor for someone else?

_____

    If you do, or are, how do you make time to spend with them? Let them know how your 40-day journey has been going.

    _____

    If you don't, ask God to bring someone who can share your desire to see blessing, can encourage you, and can help you be accountable in your commitments.

    _____

Time with God

Mark 6:30-31: *The apostles gathered around Jesus and reported to him all they had done and taught. Then, because so many people were coming and going that they did not even have a chance to eat, he said to them, "Come with me by yourselves to a quiet place and get some rest."*

Heavenly Father, give _____ the blessing of time alone with You. Orchestrate their life so there is space for them to hear from You. Issue the same invitation to _____ that You gave the disciples, "Come with me." And let them come to You with no agenda, but simply to spend time with You. Quiet, uninterrupted, intentional, focused time, prioritized for being with You. To listen, to talk, to praise, to pour out their heart in Your presence.

If _____ is not close to You now, give them a hunger and thirst, to seek You, and hear from You as they never have before. Grow in them a desire to pray and read Your Word, or get into Your amazing creation and marvel at the mountains and trees, plants and animals, moon and stars. Speak to them as only You can, in visions and dreams, through circumstances, joy and pain, opening doors for _____ to connect with You.

Because You are omnipresent, You can be with _____ at any time of day or night. Make Your presence known to them in a way that they understand they need only turn to You and speak, or cry out. Whether _____ is in need or filled with thanksgiving, let them know that You hear them and care for them.

Any time with You is time well spent. You might give _____ an answer to a specific prayer, or a revelation about Yourself. You can speak to _____ about an issue in their life, or give them a fresh perspective on something. You can provide direction or encouragement for the path they're on.

There may not be any new revelation, but just the blessing of spending restful time with their loving Father, the Almighty Creator of the universe, becoming aware of Your love for them and Your purpose for their life.

Let Time with You be a blessing from You to _____ today. Amen

Contentment

Philippians 4:12: *I know what it is to be in need, and I know what it is to have plenty. I have learned the secret of being content in any and every situation, whether well fed or hungry, whether living in plenty or in want.*

Heavenly Father, please help _____ learn what Paul learned — whether they find themselves in need or having plenty, to learn to be content in their circumstances. This can apply to money or food, the kind of home they live in, or job they have. It can deal with concerns over their body's physical appearance, mobility, strength, or level of energy. And even their relationships.

You tell us that comparing ourselves to others is a trap. Do not let _____ compare themselves to others and come away with an attitude of pride or arrogance. Or if found lacking, become filled with jealousy and covetousness. Let _____ be open to You searching and knowing their heart and removing any sinful attitude or thought.

Do not let _____ be conformed to the pattern of this world, but transform _____ by renewing their mind through Your Word and Your presence (Romans 12:2). Show them how to meet their needs in godly ways, and how to be content in all other things. Remove any desires that are ungodly. Keep _____ free from the love of money. And give them a heart of gratitude for all You have given them.

Remind _____ to bring their needs before You and wait on Your provision, trusting in Your discernment and timing.

Let Contentment be a blessing from You to _____ today. Amen

Wisdom

James 3:17: *But the wisdom that comes from heaven is first of all pure; then peace-loving, considerate, submissive, full of mercy and good fruit, impartial and sincere.*

Heavenly Father, bless _____ with Your wisdom. You tell us that heavenly wisdom comes from above. Show _____ how to seek that wisdom above all else.

Lead _____ away from "sensual wisdom" that comes from the flesh, a kind of logic based on their own thoughts or feelings. Let them realize that it leads only to self-satisfaction, pride and ultimately guilt. Shield _____ from "worldly wisdom" that is offered from people who may or may not have the knowledge or experience to be of real help. And from the pressure to seek acceptance or approval from the crowd.

Guard _____ from "demonic wisdom" that people turn to so easily today — horoscope, Tarot cards, palm readers, mediums and spiritualists. These can draw _____ into a darkness of the occult and wreak havoc in their relationships, finances, business and social life. It can bring envy, immorality, and idolatry, and can produce fear rather than any promised result.

Father, protect _____ from the deceit of the evil one, the world, and the flesh- from any who seek to deceive, swindle or mislead _____. Help _____ listen for Your voice, understand what You say, and trust in Your wisdom over what may seem right by earthly intellect. For whatever circumstances they face, give _____ that discerning ability to take what You show them and apply it to their life.

You gave wisdom to Solomon, and he was considered the wisest man in all of history. People and rulers came from all over the world to hear him speak and rule on issues for his people. Proverbs tells us we are blessed when we find wisdom, that it is more profitable than silver or gold and more precious than rubies (Proverbs 8:10-11). Enrich _____'s life with that wisdom.

Let godly Wisdom be a blessing from You to _____ today. Amen

A Grateful Heart

Psalm 100:4: *Enter his gates with thanksgiving and his courts with praise; give thanks to him and praise his name.*

Heavenly Father, show _____ how to give thanks with a grateful heart. Remind them to acknowledge You with thanks and praise for who You are and all You've done. Open their eyes so they see where You have been at work in their life. Don't let them go another day taking for granted all the gifts and blessing You've poured out on them.

Help _____ understand and make the connection that every good thing they have has come from You: their life, their health, every breath they take, the food they eat, the clothes they wear, the ability to think clearly and reason, the freedoms they enjoy, their home, job, and transportation. Help them appreciate the people in their life: loved ones, family and friends who care. And the intangible things like faith, hope, and love.

Show _____ how to express their gratitude to You, giving You the credit and thanks You deserve. Father, help _____ see the growth in their maturity, endurance and faith that has come from facing hardship, and even give You thanks for the trials and challenges. Show them how to thank You for all the times You protected them and saved them from tragedy and trauma they never even knew could have happened.

Thank You for doing what only You can do! Thank You for putting _____ in my life and for Your faithfulness in protecting them. I give You thanks, and praise Your Holy name. Let _____ rejoice in the Lord and be grateful for all Your blessings.

Let a Grateful Heart be a blessing from You to _____ today. Amen

Aaronic Blessing

Heavenly Father, as Aaron, the High Priest, gave this blessing over the people of Israel, I pray it now over _____. Defining the six Hebrew verbs adds a deeper understanding of the blessing's meaning. This expanded definition of the six Hebrew verbs in this blessing comes from Bill Bullock, The Rabbi's Son. Find him on www.biblicallifestylecenter.org

May You, Lord God, the Holy One, infuse _____ with unlimited potential and power and release them from any restrictions or limitations that would prevent them from reaching the fullness of their potential to participate in their divine purpose which You have given them.

May You zealously cherish and treasure _____, diligently defending and keeping watch over them to protect and save them.

May the light of Your innermost being and essence illuminate _____ physiologically and spiritually, impacting their body, mind, soul and spirit with Your warming, healing, soothing, restorative, empowering and constantly renewing energy.

May You, the Holy One, give _____ what they really need, not because they've earned it, or out of pity, benevolence, or even generosity, but because You have promised, as the stronger covenant partner, to strengthen _____ and enable them to reach their potential and enjoy the covenant You entered into with them, when they accepted You as Savior.

As You were face to face with the High Priest in the Holy of Holies, may You be present with _____ so they can experience true spiritual reality.

And may You place in and establish in _____, wholeness, wellness, purposeful living in joy, with abundant provision, harmony, safety, security summed up in the Hebrew word "shalom" translated "peace."

The "Priestly Blessing"

Y'varechecha Adonai
[May the Holy One bless you]

v'yish'merecha
[and zealously cherish and keep watch over you]

Ya'er Adonai panav elecha
[May the Holy One's Face shine upon you]

v'chuneka
[and shower you with grace]

Yisa Adonai panav elecha
[May the Holy One lift up His countenance upon you]

v'yasem lecha shalom
[and may He give you wholeness, wellness, security, abundant provision, and peace].

[Numbers 6:24-26]

Reflections

CONGRATULATIONS!! You made it!!

You finished the work you started! You did it! The whole 40 days!

We are so proud of you!!

How does it feel?

_____

_____

In thinking back over the prayers prayed this week . . .

>   Is there a blessing you prayed for them that you need to
>   pray for yourself?

_____

>   Pray that prayer with your own name in the blanks now.

_____

During your 40-day prayer journey, has God shown you anything
new about Himself?

_____

>   How will you apply that to your life?

_____

Have you learned anything about the one you prayed for?

_____

>   Will that change the way you think about them or interact
>   with them?

_____

Has God shown you anything new about yourself?

_____

_____

Do you feel any differently about prayer?

_____

_____

About the way God works in others?

_____

In you?

_____

Have a time of Thanksgiving! Think about these past six weeks, or the past year and give God thanks in prayer or note them here:

For the ways you've seen Him at work in your life

_____

For the things you have, and the things you don't have

_____

For the things He's allowed in your life, and those things He's protected you from

_____

For the blessing of prayer, and answers to prayers

_____

Is there someone else you can pray these 40 days of Blessing for now?

_____

Thank You After 40 Days

Heavenly Father, thank You for this journey of praying intentionally and consistently for these 40 days. Thank You for Your promise to hear me when I call to You. Do not let me forget the things I have learned about You, about prayer and about myself in these 40 days.

I pray that through these prayers for blessing, Your power will be released in _____'s life.

I continue to pray that You will make Your presence known and Your blessings felt in their life. That _____ will sense You at work, in large ways and in small ones. I am continually grateful that I can pray for You to effect Your will and Your purpose in _____'s life. I lift my prayer for You to demonstrate to _____ that through salvation and blessing, You came to bring them an abundant life!

May _____ never ever forget that You are with them and that they are Your child. May that remembrance be a powerful deterrent and an awesome reassurance. I believe Your Word will not return void, and as I have prayed Your Word and Your blessing over _____ I am trusting that it will continue to bear fruit long after these 40 days have passed.

Thank You for hearing and answering my prayers — in ways that are above and beyond what I could ever ask for or even imagine. Show me if there is someone else I can pray blessing for...even for myself. And be with me on that journey as well. Amen

Confession and Repentance

Let God speak to you now and show you any sin you need to confess. Psalm 66:18 tells us if we cherish sin in our hearts, God won't listen to our prayers. Tell God you are willing to turn away from those things (which is repentance) and ask for His forgiveness.

1 John 1:9-10 tells us, "If we confess our sins, He is faithful and righteous to forgive us our sins and to cleanse us from all unrighteousness. If we claim we have not sinned, we make Him a liar, and His word is not in us."

Ask God if there are sins of:

THOUGHT — impure, selfish, angry, fearful, jealous

ATTITUDE — prideful, judgmental, argumentative, lukewarm toward God

SPEECH — crude, inappropriate, grumbling, divisive, lies, half-truths

RELATIONSHIP — wrong or improper, physically or emotionally
Do you need to forgive someone? Do you need to ask for forgiveness?
As a husband: are you providing spiritual leadership, guiding, and nurturing your wife?
As a wife: are you honoring and respecting your husband?
As parents: are you modeling godly behavior and attitudes and teaching your children in love?
As children or teens: are you respectful and obedient?

COMMISSION — things that you have done, actions you have taken
Have you done something you know is wrong?
Do you guard your eyes?
Have you exposed yourself to the occult?
Do you have habits that are harmful to your body — mind — spirit?

OMISSION — things you have failed to do
Has God prompted you to do something you haven't done?
Have you failed to do good when you could have?
SELF-RULE — rebellion, going your own way

Are you following God or going your own way?
Are you avoiding something He's told you to do?
Or are you still doing something He's told you not to?

Spiritual Armor for Battle

Ephesians 6:10-18: *Finally, be strong in the Lord and in his mighty power. Put on the full armor of God, so that you can take your stand against the devil's schemes. For our struggle is not against flesh and blood, but against the rulers, against the authorities, against the powers of this dark world and against the spiritual forces of evil in the heavenly realms. Therefore put on the full armor of God, so that when the day of evil comes, you may be able to stand your ground, and after you have done everything, to stand. Stand firm then, with the belt of truth buckled around your waist, with the breastplate of righteousness in place, and with your feet fitted with the readiness that comes from the gospel of peace. In addition to all this, take up the shield of faith, with which you can extinguish all the flaming arrows of the evil one. Take the helmet of salvation and the sword of the Spirit, which is the word of God.*

And pray in the Spirit on all occasions with all kinds of prayers and requests. With this in mind, be alert and always keep on praying for all the Lord's people.

We dress ourselves in the armor that Paul describes here. He wrote his letter to the Ephesians while he was in Rome, under house arrest, guarded by Roman soldiers. Every day, he saw men dressed in armor, bearing the insignia of their authority. The Holy Spirit must have inspired his analogy of a Christian "soldier."

Praying on the armor can be as simple as listing each piece and stating that you are putting it on and wearing it.

When we are praying for someone, or even ourselves, the devil doesn't like it. And even with his limited power here on earth, we can find ourselves under attack in ways that can lead us to feel discouraged, defeated, even want to give up.

But we rely on the fact that God's armor is the very best!

The **Belt of Truth** is a wide, tight band around the waist that holds pieces of the armor on, as well as the sword. When we are wearing truth we can more easily recognize the lies the devil would tempt us to believe. We will not be mesmerized by half-truths or deceptions.

The **Breastplate of Righteousness** protects our heart and vital organs, a kind of forerunner of the bulletproof vest. It stops and deflects stabs and projectiles. Our righteousness comes from Jesus Christ. His blood paid the price for our sin and we gain the righteousness of the perfect life He lived. In that righteousness the devil cannot hold anything against us.

The **Shoes of the Gospel of Peace** will help us walk in the Spirit. Putting on shoes is a sign of readiness and preparedness. With these we are ready to carry the Good News of salvation and peace into our relationships and whatever challenges we face. With our feet protected like this we will have traction even when we feel unsteady, and will be able to stand firm.

The **Shield of Faith** is not some puny little garbage can lid with a handle, but a head to toe protection, repelling the enemy's offensive weapons. When the shield was anointed with oil it would reflect the glare of the sun and blind the enemy. This shield covered a soldier from top to bottom, side to side and can join with others to form a wall of protection that will fend off an attacker while advancing in the field of battle.

Our faith in God protects us when the world or others tells us things are hopeless or cannot work out because we have the One True God who is all-knowing and all-powerful. We trust in His love for us and know that He has a plan for us, to give us hope and a future with Him in eternity. Every time He keeps a promise, or delivers us from some trouble, or stands with us in hardship, it builds or faith—strengthens our shields! And when we stand beside other believers in their faith, we are protected even more!

The **Helmet of Salvation** protects our head and identifies who we fight for. This helmet also protects our minds and helps guard our thoughts. The enemy would want to fill our minds with thoughts of doubt, fear and insecurity. But when thoughts and emotional responses are stirred up, we can hold them up to the light of truth: scripture. God's Word is the truth that will combat all that would discourage us.

And the **Sword of the Spirit** is God's Word, and strikes at the lies the devil would use to try and defeat us. We can use it to refute any lies the devil tries to get us to believe. We can pray it as part of our prayers. We can speak it out loud as an attack on the enemy. There is power in the Word of God.

Here is a sample prayer:

Heavenly Father, I come before you with thanks for the armor that You give me, which is the best. With the belt of truth fastened around my waist, I say that I will not believe the lies the devil would try to use to confuse me. Give me clarity and understanding. Help me see past what the world and others would tell me, to what you want to say to me.

I wear the helmet of salvation to guard my mind, and I take every thought captive to You. The breastplate of righteousness I place over my chest to protect my heart.

I wear the shoes of peace to say that I am ready to hear from You and to obey what You tell me to do.

I take up my shield to repel all the arguments the evil one would send against me. And I take up the sword, the Word of God, as a weapon to help me stand firm against the devil's schemes.

Thank you for hearing my prayer. Amen.

APPENDIX C

Hearing from God

Proverbs 8:32-5: *Now then, my children, listen to me;*
blessed are those who keep my ways.
Listen to my instruction and be wise;
do not disregard it.
Blessed are those who listen to me,
watching daily at my doors,
waiting at my doorway.
For those who find me find life
and receive favor from the LORD.

But how do I know if what I hear is from God or some other voice??

When you believe you've heard from God You, write it down and put it to the test.

Ask these three questions to see if you heard it from God or some other source:

1 — Does what I hear agree with the Bible?
The answer must be "yes." God will never tell you anything that contradicts what He has already said in His Word. So, spend time in and be familiar with the Bible.

If you need help, a Christian friend or pastor can help you find scripture dealing with your topic. If there is nothing, or you are unsure, ask God to reveal the truth to you.

One role of the Holy Spirit who dwells in every believer is to teach us, guiding us in truth. In John 14:26, Jesus tells us the Holy Spirit will teach us all things. And in John 16:13 tells us the Holy Spirit will guide us into all truth.

2 — Will the result, or the fruit of the act be the fruit of the Spirit?
This answer should also be "yes." The result of what you hear should lead to and produce the fruit of the Spirit in your life and those around you.

Galatians 5:19-23 outlines the fruit of the Spirit as: love, joy, peace, patience, kindness, goodness, faithfulness, gentleness, and self-control.

Verses 19-12 tell us the acts of the flesh are immorality, impurity, debauchery, idolatry, witchcraft, hatred, discord, jealousy, rage, selfish ambition, dissension, envy, and the like.

So if you act on what you think God is telling you, what will happen? Look at the expected result, or the "fruit," to see where it leads.

3 — Will it benefit my relationship with God?

Again, **this answer should be "yes."** Everything you do will benefit or weaken your relationship with God.

Micah 6:8 *And what does the LORD require of you? To act justly and to love mercy and to walk humbly with your God.*

Most of the time, the Holy Spirit will tell you if what you are doing is pulling you away from God. You will probably be able to sense that you are either drawing closer to God or pulling away if you were to follow through on what you think you hear Him telling you.

It might help to ask another Christian friend, pastor or counselor. Or even pose the question: What Would Jesus do?

If you hit a "no" stop right there! What you heard is **NOT from God**. If it
does NOT agree with the Bible, or
does NOT produce the Fruit of the Spirit, or
does NOT benefit your relationship with God,
then it is NOT from God.

So what do you do ?

If you got a NO —

Pray for strength to say "no" to that and keep seeking God's wisdom.

James 1:5 says, *"If any of you lacks wisdom, you should ask God, who gives generously to all without finding fault, and it will be given to you."* So ask again for God's input.

If you got 3 YES —

Pray for the strength and courage to follow through on what God has shown you.

Paul encourages us that we can do all things through Christ who strengthens us (Philippians 4:13).

If confusion still exists, go back and ask God for clarity. And be patient. The answer may be unclear because the timing isn't right. Be willing to wait on God's timing.

Psalm 27:14: *Wait for the LORD; be strong and take heart and wait for the LORD.*

Hearing from God Worksheet

Is what I'm hearing from God?

James 1:5 *If any of you lacks wisdom, you should ask God, who gives generously to all without finding fault, and it will be given to you.*

If you hit a "No" stop there. Is it NOT from God.

What is my concern or question
What am I hearing?
What does the Bible say about my concern and what I am hearing?
Does what I am hearing agree with the Bible? ❑Y ❑N
If I act on what I've heard, what will it produce in my life and others?
Is that a Fruit of the Spirit? ❑Y ❑N
If I act on what I've heard, will it benefit my relationship with God? ❑Y ❑N

About the Authors

Eric Sprinkle: A former Whitewater Guide and Swift-water Rescue Instructor for the U.S. military, Eric travels the country speaking about the benefits of risk, managing fear, and how to make life more exciting by "living a slightly more dangerous lifestyle." He calls the multi-sport playground of Colorado Springs home and desperately needs any book series that can help him pray more intentionally.

Laura Shaffer: An Army Brat moving almost every year till college, Laura was delighted to discover that wherever she went, God was always there ahead of her. Even though the houses, and friends changed, there was always Sunday School and church where she learned that God was always with her. And she felt it.

Through the years she continued in her awareness of God's presence, especially working in the yard and taking nature walks in beautiful, colorful, Colorado. She writes to encourage people to lean into God and learn from Him in their daily life through nature, scripture, circumstances and prayer.

And now she wants to help you experience God's presence - equipping you to pray more intentionally and consistently, to empower your prayer life, and deepen your relationship with God.

Check out Laura's blog at www.DailyBiblePrayer.wordpress.com for scripture-based examples of her prayers anytime.

Additional Thoughts on Praying Blessings

More from Adventure Experience Press

Adventure Devos: The first devotional written exclusively for men with a heart for Risk and Danger

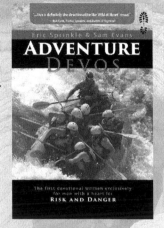

Adventure Devos: Women's Edition: An exciting devotional written exclusively for women with a Heart for Risk and Adventure

Adventure Devos: Youth Edition: Summer Camp never has to end when your devotional takes you adventuring all year long!

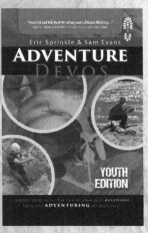

Made in the USA
Columbia, SC
23 November 2021